the things
i ~~can't~~ say

the things
i ~~can't~~ say

brianna sparks

the things i can't say
by Brianna Sparks.
Independently Published, 2023

ISBN - 9798863806297

to those
whose true emotions are
buried deep

...

I dream of a time I can look into your eyes and say these words, telling you how I truly feel.

But for now, I hope to heal my broken heart, I hope to forgive those who hurt me, I hope to find true love and friendship, I hope to ease my grieving process and get through my lowest point to find healing. But most of all, I hope I find true happiness along the way.

These are the words that truly describes my inner emotions and I hope it resonates with you.

ABOUT THE BOOK

In this book the author talks about her feelings and thoughts on aspects of true emotions. She dives deep sharing her true feelings on love, heartbreak, healing, grief, depression, friendship, trust, forgiveness and happiness. With each aspect comes raw emotions penned on paper in a poetic style. Through the course of reading this book, we hope you see through her eyes and heart as it evokes deep aspect of your emotions buried deep.

feelings from the heart

the feelings left unexpressed are the ones that carry the true emotions

How I Feel About Love

sometimes i'm confused about the true meaning of love, is it about putting others before yourself or knowing when to prioritize what's best for you before everything else? is it knowing how much you mean to someone, enough to take a walk when you know you deserve better?

can you love someone else and love yourself in the process or there's only room for one? because i feel true love means knowing you mean the world to a person that brings out the best version of you.

THE THINGS I CAN'T SAY

love doesn't have to be so hard
you know it's worth it
when you can find true happiness

HOW I FEEL ABOUT LOVE

i'm learning to love you, to experience what it truly means to be loved by a person. i'm learning to know i have the best person in the world by my side till forever. but most of all, i'm learning to love myself in the process of loving you. i hope you're patient enough to hold my hand through it all.

THE THINGS I CAN'T SAY

i can assure you one thing
i'll be there for you
through thick and thin
even when everyone else leaves
it's just going to be you and me

HOW I FEEL ABOUT LOVE

if i say i love you, know it's real. i love you with all my heart and everything in-between. i would risk it all for you in a heartbeat and take on the wildest adventure just to be with you. i would move mountains and cross stormy seas just to be by your side. i would love you even at my lowest point because you made loving you, a very easy thing for me to do.

THE THINGS I CAN'T SAY

i'm learning to love myself
while loving you
because it takes the bravest heart
to love two at a time

love doesn't have to make you lose yourself. it is meant to help you discover your true feelings, passion and desires. it is meant to help you learn what makes the best version of who you are. it is meant to bring out your inner child and help you feel secure even at your lowest points. love isn't only meant to make you feel complete but also to bring out the parts of you that you didn't know exists.

THE THINGS I CAN'T SAY

falling in love with you
was the beautiful "change"
i never knew i needed

you came in and changed my whole world

you made falling in love with you so natural and seamless. it's a beautiful feeling, one i can't explain. it's like finding the right answers to my lifelong questions while unraveling the pieces of puzzle to my heart. you make me feel vulnerable yet so secure at the same time. being loved by you is truly a blessing. it has helped me realize the parts of me i didn't even know exists. it made me become a better version of myself and it made me realize love doesn't have to hurt.

surely loving you has brought me so much joy
but being loved by you is the true blessing.

THE THINGS I CAN'T SAY

i'm not scared of falling in love
i'm just worried
i might fall for the wrong person

HOW I FEEL ABOUT LOVE

love shouldn't just be based on romance, late nights out or sex. it should so be much more. it should be about building special bonds and connections you can't share with anyone else but them. it should be about commitment, tolerance and acceptance.
love shouldn't just be a word but an wholesome experience.

THE THINGS I CAN'T SAY

i'm glad we met when we did
because i can't picture anything else
without you in it

HOW I FEEL ABOUT LOVE

i'm grateful we found love in our time, we found a love that wasn't rushed or forced. a love that only we understood. we slowly got to know each other, unraveling every piece of each other's heart. we figured out our deepest secrets, fears, desires and passion. we found each other's flaws but accepted we weren't perfect. we fought for what we had and faced everything life threw at us. our arms became each other's safe space and comfort zone. we became each other's home and happy place. love became the only language our hearts understood and the only rhythm it beats to.

i'm glad we found each other
love found us when we needed it the most

THE THINGS I CAN'T SAY

i love the idea of "being in love" with you
it calms my soul and soothes my spirit

How I Feel About Heartbreak

HOW I FEEL ABOUT HEARTBREAK

why do i still feel like it's all a dream. why does it hurt just thinking about it. i thought we were each other's magic tale. our together forever kind of fairytale. i thought we said we would have each other's back and face everything life throws at us. when did everything take a turn downhill. when did we cease to become each other's highlight of the day. or maybe it's just you.

for you're still my person
this timeline and the next

THE THINGS I CAN'T SAY

i can only tell the tale of how we fell in love
but not how we fell out of it
because even though you left
i'm still here loving you everyday

as the memories flood in, i can't help but think, was it all not meant to be? was our paths crossing just meant to teach us how a love that isn't meant to be feels? or maybe we cracked up our fireworks way too soon, maybe the ink to write our story dried up even before we picked the book. maybe, just maybe we could have danced slowly to the tunes of love or maybe our story was meant to be an almost right from the start.

THE THINGS I CAN'T SAY

they say fall in love with someone
who loves you for 'who you are'
but what happens when you fall in love
with someone who makes 'being you'
the hardest thing to do

HOW I FEEL ABOUT HEARTBREAK

a letter to my once true love

as we bring the chapter we started to a close, here are a few things i need you to know.

i'm glad you were part of my story even if it didn't end in forever. you made my time with you an amazing experience even if it wasn't for you. you've made me truly appreciate how much i've grown, enough to know it's time to take a walk. i'm glad to have experienced love with you while your heart was still with me. i appreciate you for holding my hand even though it slipped away.

it's going to be a hard one from here now but i have to let you go, because if you were truly meant to be mine it wouldn't have hurt the way it did.

you were my easiest hello but my hardest goodbye

THE THINGS I CAN'T SAY

in the end i realized
you didn't hurt me
"i did"

i allowed myself to get lost
in the process of loving you

HOW I FEEL ABOUT HEARTBREAK

it's raining heavy outside
pelting down so hard
but my heart is heavier

i remember those times we would lay next to each
other listening to the sounds of thunder while
planning our future all at once. it was one of those
times i felt closest to you. those times we would talk
about our plans and aspirations for the future,
chattering away about sweet nothings while joking
around about how cute we'll look when we grew
older.

who would have thought we wouldn't even finish the
present. who would have thought our flaming love
would ever run cold, and who would have thought i'll
grow old with only the memories of how we pictured
it all to be.

THE THINGS I CAN'T SAY

THE THINGS I CAN'T SAY

maybe we weren't meant to work out
as much as we want it to

HOW I FEEL ABOUT HEARTBREAK

you filled up the lines
in my empty love story
until your ink dried out

now all i'm left with
is a half written love tale

unable to complete, impossible to erase

THE THINGS I CAN'T SAY

the reality of heartbreak hits
when you are stuck waiting for them
and unable to move on

HOW I FEEL ABOUT HEARTBREAK

i wouldn't call our time together a waste, it really was that time of our lives when we didn't know better. it was that time we were trying to figure out ourselves individually while learning to love each other. it was that phase we could have proven how much we loved each other, but i know i did. i gave it my all even while it hurt, i gave my all and it drained me. you didn't even try to fight for us or what we shared. you gave up all we had without looking back. but now i know what really went wrong, i was never enough for you right from the very start.

THE THINGS I CAN'T SAY

i guess we can both agree
on one thing
it was fun
while it lasted

HOW I FEEL ABOUT HEARTBREAK

i'm here wondering if loving you should hurt this much. if choosing to be by your side was my greatest mistake. if losing myself was the price i had to pay just to be called "yours".

but i've come to realize why it hurt
it was because i chose to remain

i chose to be blinded by the idea of "being in love". i chose not to see how you broke me constantly and apologized, how you failed to respect me or what we had. you continuously made me feel less loved, less appreciated and ignored. you made a mockery of my feelings with your actions and how you treated me. until i finally realized how broken I was and how loving you wasn't enough to make you love me back.

THE THINGS I CAN'T SAY

loving you was probably the easiest
and the hardest thing to do
at the same time

HOW I FEEL ABOUT HEARTBREAK

perhaps we were meant to find each other
in another timeline but not this
perhaps we weren't meant to find ourselves
in this universe but in the parallel one

because now that we've found each other
in the same universe
it seems to be a different timeline
that would never work

THE THINGS I CAN'T SAY

i guess we both lied
you lied you'll always be mine
and i lied i'll never fall for you

but the truth is

i fell for you
but you were never mine

HOW I FEEL ABOUT HEARTBREAK

yesterday was your birthday
that's a special day
we always got to celebrate together
i wanted to text you
to shower you with praises
like i always did
but then it hit me
i've been replaced
and my text would probably be lost
in their "i love you's"

THE THINGS I CAN'T SAY

i fucking loved you!
more than i loved myself
and i guess
that's what broke me the most
when you decided to leave

HOW I FEEL ABOUT HEARTBREAK

i know it's over but it's hard to accept it, it's hard to know we are nothing but in the past now. i want to put this all behind me but it's hard to do. it's hard to forget how sweet my name sounded when you called it. it's hard to forget how the smell of the sheets reminds me of you. it's hard to forget how your smile lit up my mood and how your arms felt like my safe space. it's hard to erase your whole existence in my world because everything in it reminds me of you.

you'll always be a constant reminder
of how i found love and how i lost it

THE THINGS I CAN'T SAY

if i could summarise
our love story in a sentence
it would be-

"so much love given, so much love lost"

our favourite song is one i can't listen to anymore. i can't stop by at our favourite spot because of the memories it holds. i can't say some words out loud as they were our favourite way of communicating and i dare not say your name else i'll cry myself to sleep. my heart is filled with broken promises and shattered dreams of our perfect together-forever fairytale.

THE THINGS I CAN'T SAY

let me live in this world i created for myself
it's the world of make believes
because only then do you exist

as "mine" -

HOW I FEEL ABOUT HEARTBREAK

my friends told me to stop this cycle i find myself in,
the cycle of blocking just to unblock you again.
but guess what? i can't stop myself.
i'm here wondering how much you've been able to
move on from "us". i find myself taking sneak peeks
at your recent post maybe i could find an element of
what's left of us. or maybe you've found a new life
that doesn't involve me in it. maybe it was easy for
you to replace me or what we had. or maybe i wasn't
who you wanted after all.

but i keep asking myself

why do i care so much. why do i care about someone
who doesn't care about my feelings. or maybe you
didn't care as much as i hoped you would. maybe i
set the standard so high for you to attain, or maybe i
deserve so much more than you could ever give.
but one thing i've learnt is never to settle

because what's fit for me
will always find me

THE THINGS I CAN'T SAY

i kept pouring myself out to you
draining every last drop
just to please you
until i ran out
with nothing left to give

HOW I FEEL ABOUT HEARTBREAK

i caught a glimpse of you the other day
with your "she's only just a friend'
i wanted to say hello
to prove to you i wasn't overreacting
like you always said i was
but i realized at that moment
my decision to walk away
was for the best
because i knew i deserved better
i deserved so much more
than you could ever give

THE THINGS I CAN'T SAY

if i had to tell a tale about love
i'll tell them all about you
because you were love itself to me
even if i wasn't for you

HOW I FEEL ABOUT HEARTBREAK

love used to be only just word
until i met you
and heartbreak was only just a word
until i lost you

now i understand the true meaning of both

THE THINGS I CAN'T SAY

we deliberately chose
to destroy "our forever"
now it's a beautiful dream -

one that no longer exists

HOW I FEEL ABOUT HEARTBREAK

i would miss you a lot you know

i'd miss the early morning banter over coffee or tea. i'd miss the way you called my name while you walk in. i'd miss the random "i love you' pop ups on my phone that brightens up my day. i'd miss the tight hugs and cuddle from behind while fixing dinner. i'd miss the late night talks and plans about our future and how we wanted to see the world together. i'd miss the fights and arguments about the dumbest things because only then did we get to understand each other more. i'd miss how we brought joyful colors to each other's world even though it's all gray now.

but what i would miss the most
is how i can no longer call you "mine"

THE THINGS I CAN'T SAY

our time together
taught me so many things
it taught me that being a good woman
isn't enough for a man
who isn't ready to commit to one

How I Feel About Healing

HOW I FEEL ABOUT HEALING

i'm afraid i might not heal
or is it the fear of healing
that scares me
because i know once healing comes
what matters most to me now
might mean nothing to me soon

THE THINGS I CAN'T SAY

THE THINGS I CAN'T SAY

learn to let go of your past trauma
because holding on just makes it
a million times worse

when healing finds you, there would be no late night tears. the ray of sunshine through your window wouldn't hurt your eyes anymore. your mornings would be brighter and better and you'll appreciate being alive. your dried up roses would begin to bloom again and the chirpy sounds of nature would be melodious to your healing heart. you would look at the mirror and appreciate being free, free of the burden and guilt that once consumed you. you would be eager to face the day with so much joy and hope. hope of finding your dreams, desires and true self. your nights would be filled with fulfillment and contentment.

but most of all, your gray world would be full of rainbows.

when healing finds you...

THE THINGS I CAN'T SAY

you begin to heal
when you let everything else go

HOW I FEEL ABOUT HEALING

the journey to healing wouldn't be a jolly ride. there would be days you just want to drop off without getting to your destination. tears of pain, sadness and regret would stream down your cheeks. you would close your eyes and wish for it to all go away but it wouldn't, and that's okay.

it's okay to go through all the aspects of your emotions. it's okay to blame yourself and the decisions you've made that got you here. it's okay to be vulnerable, remorseful and broken.

it's okay to acknowledge your faults and take responsibiliy for your actions. it's a step towards healing. the pain and hurt would ease after a while. you would learn from your mistakes and it would help you discover a better version of yourself. you would learn to let it all go and peace would be your only forte.

healing might take a while, but it would surely come.

THE THINGS I CAN'T SAY

the best path to healing
is to let go of the grudges

only then can you truly be free

HOW I FEEL ABOUT HEALING

learn to appreciate your healing journey
all that matter is you getting through
each day at a time

THE THINGS I CAN'T SAY

i've told myself over and over again
that being away from you
is the best way to find 'me'
that allowing you back in
would only destroy me
in ways i can't even explain

i guess this time i'll get the courage
to move on and heal
because i can't continue this crazy cycle
of tormenting my soul

How I Feel About Depression

HOW I FEEL ABOUT DEPRESSION

i wouldn't say i'm happy, i wouldn't say i'm sad. i feel i'm just in-between the two worlds yet so close to one. sometimes i feel so excited, so happy to begin my day. then i'm hit with the wave of sadness, one i can't explain. maybe it's the pain, maybe it's the trauma buried deep.

i'm excited this moment
and i'm sobbing the next

i can never understand the reason why

THE THINGS I CAN'T SAY

being at your lowest point
isn't the worst thing
but being stuck with no way out
is the scariest part

HOW I FEEL ABOUT DEPRESSION

i found myself asking these questions over and over again without finding any answers. the truth is no-one could really answer them for me. no one could really see the depth of how broken i was. was i okay like i told everyone i was? was i really fine deep inside like i pretended to be? was i ever going to find happiness and the love i once knew?

i kept asking till i found the answers that never came

THE THINGS I CAN'T SAY

i swear "i'm okay"
fuck it! i'm not!

HOW I FEEL ABOUT DEPRESSION

i was once a happy child
beaming in the love and affection
showered upon me
by those i believed so much in
i lived in a fantasy world
of roses and petals
devoid of thorns
or so i thought

i failed to realize
winter was around the corner
and my roses and petals froze in time

THE THINGS I CAN'T SAY

cry your eyes out while you can
because the moment you cry
without dropping a single tear
then you know
you're truly at rock bottom

HOW I FEEL ABOUT DEPRESSION

i'm being sucked into this rapid sinking hole. unable to get out, unable to cry for help. i keep up the facade that i have it all under control but deep inside i'm crashing. i'm shattering and crumbling from within. i may tell you i'm doing great but i'm really not.

i'm okay seems to be the default answer
when you're truly far from it

THE THINGS I CAN'T SAY

i used to be a people pleaser
until i learnt
the more you please people
the less appreciated your efforts are

HOW I FEEL ABOUT DEPRESSION

some say depression
is a feeling of emptiness
that makes you ball your eyes out
but i say it's depression
when you cry but no single tear drops

THE THINGS I CAN'T SAY

what depression means to me

D- deep
E- emotions
P- put
R- repeatedly
E- every
S- single
S- second
I- into
O- obvious
N- nothingness

HOW I FEEL ABOUT DEPRESSION

depression is now a word being thrown around without it being fully understood. it has become just a common saying to justify momentary sadness.
but the truth is

it's a mixed feeling of different emotions all at once.

it's feeling happy-sad-happy-angry-hopeful and back to sadness all in a split second.
the truth remains-

you don't know how deep you are in it
until you start sinking.

THE THINGS I CAN'T SAY

let's play pretend
let's pretend i'm okay
no one would really know if i'm not right?

but the truth is no one really cares

let's pretend that i'm dying
they'll care then i guess?

it's still the same- no one cares!

let's pretend i'm famous
maybe it'll get their attention?

*they - "let's pretend we love her then use it to
our advantage"*

so drop the pretend game and be yourself
because pleasing people would only leave you
miserable and drained

How I Feel About Grief

i remember our last hug, our last conversation, our last goodbye. what hurts the most is not knowing at the time it would be out last, maybe we could have talked a little longer, maybe i wouldn't let go of the hug as fast as i did and maybe i wouldn't have been able to bring myself to say goodbye because knowing i can never have those moments back breaks my heart.

THE THINGS I CAN'T SAY

the true actions that hurt
are the ones that never happened
the true words that hurt
are the ones that were never said
the true feelings that hurt
are the ones left unexpressed

HOW I FEEL ABOUT GRIEF

i'm here wishing i did one last thing
whispered in your ears
how much you mean to me
hoping i gave you my all
while you were still here with me
but all i'm left with is wishes
for you're no longer by my side
but you'll always be in my heart

THE THINGS I CAN'T SAY

the worst kind of grief
is missing someone
who is right next to you
because they may be right there
but not present with you at heart.

HOW I FEEL ABOUT GRIEF

no one stays with you forever
only memories will

be there for whom you care about
because you don't know how soon
they'll belong to the past

HOW I FEEL ABOUT GRIEF

you promised to stay forever

why then did you leave

now all i have of you is-
MEMORIES

how do i cope?

THE THINGS I CAN'T SAY

grieving for someone who's still alive
has to be the hardest thing to do
because even though they are right there
they are still out of reach

How I Feel About Friendship

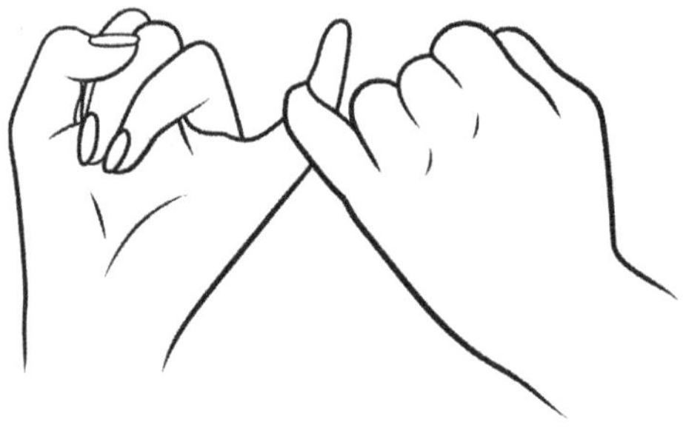

HOW I FEEL ABOUT FRIENDSHIP

to my one true friend

thank you for being a constant in my life's crazy equation. thank you for being a controlled experiment to my scientific life story. thank you for being my anchor at my lowest points. thank you for proving to be the best friend anyone can ask for. thank you for being different from everyone and everything else. but most of all, thank you for being your true self through it all.

THE THINGS I CAN'T SAY

THE THINGS I CAN'T SAY

"friend" isn't just a word
it's the loyalty that comes
with being one

HOW I FEEL ABOUT FRIENDSHIP

i would be your alarm system
when trouble comes
and your support system
to get you out of it

THE THINGS I CAN'T SAY

be with friends who see the best in you
and what you're becoming
not the ones who see the worst in you
and what you could have been

HOW I FEEL ABOUT FRIENDSHIP

i'm that one friend you can count on
the one that's going to have your back
even when everything else falls apart
i'll be there to hold your hands
and together we will pick up the pieces
and make it whole again

THE THINGS I CAN'T SAY

if you love me at my worst
and then hate me at my best
you're just a friendly reminder
that i don't give a fuck!

HOW I FEEL ABOUT FRIENDSHIP

they say meeting a genuine and true friend
is like searching a haystack of garbage
for a piece of diamond
the chances of finding it
is rare-

but not impossible

THE THINGS I CAN'T SAY

it's a different kind of feeling
knowing you have that one person
that's going to have your back
even at your worst life decisions

HOW I FEEL ABOUT FRIENDSHIP

surround yourself
with positive people
delete the negative ones

repeat-

THE THINGS I CAN'T SAY

true friendship
doesn't only mean "ride or die"
it means being ready to die
even before the ride

How I Feel About Forgiveness

HOW I FEEL ABOUT FORGIVENESS

if i was asked about our time together, i wouldn't have anything bad to say. i would tell all about those beautiful mornings waking up next to you that made it feel like home. i would tell them of the journey to find true love even if it wasn't meant to last till forever. i would tell them of the path i found to love myself while being in love with you. because even though i was hurt in the process of loving you, it led me to discover, accept and forgive myself.

and that's the true blessing i found

i hope it was worth every drop of my tear. i hope it was worth the pain we both went through. i hope your decision to leave was best for you even if you didn't care how i felt. i hope you find the happiness i could no longer give.
i forgive you.

i hope forgiveness is enough to find my peace

HOW I FEEL ABOUT FORGIVENESS

forgiving them
doesn't make you look weak
it means you're strong enough
to realize
what would help you heal

forgive yourself-
it's the first step towards healing

How I Feel About Happiness

HOW I FEEL ABOUT HAPPINESS

i'm happy because i "choose" to be
not because i "want" to be
that's being intentional

read again -

THE THINGS I CAN'T SAY

being happy isn't just a word
it's a state of mind
when you're at peace with yourself

How I Feel About Trust

HOW I FEEL ABOUT TRUST

i'll take my time to understand and figure out what makes you happy or sad, what makes you tick or mad. i'll be the best i can, a lover, a companion and a true friend. i'll be loyal, attentive and i'll always look out for you.

but the truth is -

i'll expect some level of commitment. i'll expect my efforts to be reciprocated. i'll believe i can trust and rely on you when i'm at my lowest.

the truth remains -

once that level of trust is broken, i'll find it hard to move on from that.

i'm the type with a fragile heart. one that gets hurt easily, one that's afraid of being judged or misunderstood. my safe place is in my head. i prefer to be in company of myself rather than being with anyone else. but i do love, i do care and i do trust. i'll take my time to observe and slowly let you in. once you are in, you'll understand how sweet and vulnerable i can be. once i let you in, know that you're one of the few i trust so dearly.

i hope that trust is never broken

...

Welcome to the beginning of a new chapter. I hope by now you can find the right words to describe your feelings. I hope you can tell others how you truly feel without the fear of being judged or hurt. I hope you find the courage from now on to face your true fears.

best wishes,
Brianna

About the author

Brianna is a free spirited cabin lover who enjoys nature and serenity. She finds solace in peace and quiet where she's able to process her emotions enough to pen them on paper.

She loves reading books, keeping journals and writing poetry. Her love for poetry started way back in high school and developed through college years. "The things I can't say" is a collection of her thoughts and emotions through different stages of her life .

This is her debut shot into the world of poetry.

Find me on socials

Instagram- briannasparkspoetry
Tiktok- briannasparkspoetry
Email- briannasparkspoetry@gmail.com

Made in the USA
Monee, IL
17 July 2024